A HEART'S LANDSCAPE

A HEART'S LANDSCAPE

An Invitation to the
Garden of Moments

SUSAN LAX

Your Moment Press

Published by Your Moment Press, New York
https://www.emailforyoursoul.com

Edited and designed by Girl Friday Productions
www.girlfridayproductions.com

Design: Paul Barrett
Editorial: Bethany Davis
Project management: Sara Spees Addicott

Image credits: cover © Shutterstock/soft_light; interior images courtesy of the author

ISBN (hardcover): 978-0-578-96294-8

Library of Congress Control Number: 2021921122

First edition

For you: I love you more than the whole world and back again, and more than that . . .

INTRODUCTION

How This Book Came to Be

When I reached the age of fifty, my life began to change. Until then, I had positioned myself comfortably as a mother and spouse. I was also a teacher, a dedicated activist, and a volunteer. I had a successful business and had even gone back to school to study my passion for lessons of the heart, healing, and spiritual growth.

Yet it was in the roles of parenting and spousehood where I found my identity. I had long ago fallen in love with motherhood, partnership, and the creation of a family. This was *where* I saw myself; this was *how* I saw myself.

Shortly before my fiftieth birthday, the movie *Mamma Mia* was released, and I was excited to go see it. There was a scene where the main character, played by Meryl Streep, and her friends were jumping on the bed. I remember it vividly, watching with great enthusiasm and placing the scene in my heart memory. I shared my girlish delight with Steven, my partner in life and love. I envisioned being somewhere serene with my girlfriends, the women in my life, all of us jumping on a bed, singing, dancing, celebrating.

Amazingly, this all became a reality when Steven and my three daughters organized a surprise birthday trip to Santorini for a week with the precious women in my life. For seven days, I was showered with love, laughter, and the joyhood of friendship, inviting me to softly open the windows of my soul. And yes, we did indeed have that delightful jumping-on-the-bed moment.

My fiftieth birthday gifted me with much more than a giddy jumping-on-the-bed moment, though; it gifted me with a renewed sense of self-awareness. I came away from that trip knowing more about Susan, the woman inside me, than I had ever known before.

That trip planted many seeds in the garden of my spirit—a garden that would bloom with the colors of intimacy with myself as well as others. I had discovered the strength of female friendships, the art of receiving, and the powerful gifts of sisterhood.

Stephanie was one of my friends who had shared in that unique Santorini bonding experience. Our daughters had been close friends for eleven years. We followed in their footsteps, creating a friendship of our own, one that was nurtured by weekly phone calls filled with everyday chat and heart talk. We had grown up in two different countries, with two different cultures. I learned from her and she from me, but it was our love of laughter that truly connected us.

Then, one day, cancer entered Stephanie's life, causing our communication to go silent as she focused on trying to heal. While honoring the sacredness of her privacy, I wanted to find a way to bring voice back to our bond. So, each morning at six o'clock, I would send Stephanie a short email, with the hope that my words might offer her a moment of joy as she faced yet another challenging twenty-four hours. We never exchanged vocal words about these emails. I just assured her no reply was expected, and if she requested the emails to stop, they would, no questions asked.

Every morning I wrote of her courage and resilience, not her illness. My hands typed words of mundane moments, eager to remind her heart of the world outside of cancer. Although we spoke over the phone, we never mentioned my early-morning emails in the space of our conversation.

About five months into my email messaging, on a random weekday, the flu captured my health, preventing me from sending Stephanie my morning words. At approximately 7:30 a.m., I received an unexpected call. Slightly feverish, I was startled by Stephanie's recognizable voice.

"Where is my morning blessing? Why didn't you send it today?"

Unbeknownst to me, an effort to hold her hand from afar had become an important part of her morning routine. From then on, my "morning blessings" continued to find their way to Stephanie for the remaining year. I journeyed through them and with them to her in-box as she healed.

Sitting at my desk each morning, I slowly discovered an ability to translate my heart words into written ones. As time went by, I began to see how my "morning blessings" might also open new pathways for me to reach and inspire the women I worked with as a spiritual counselor.

This is how my "morning blessings" to Stephanie gave birth to "Morning Inspiration." A daily email for the soul, it was one I would share every morning with women residing in the house of healing. Many of these women were also riding the wave of a cancerous ocean with passionate bravery. At a moment when newly born courageousness was needed, Morning Inspiration waited for them. Some swam into the arms of remission; others were softly carried by the sea of heaven.

Remission's embrace welcomed Stephanie; she carries her badge of a cancer thriver with pride.

Thereafter, Morning Inspiration generated an energy of its own. I began to receive emails from women around the world requesting to be put on the list. I never asked them, nor do I ask today, how they discovered Morning Inspiration. Perhaps it is the way of the universe that when we are ready to receive what we need, it finds us.

The expanding interest took me by surprise. As more men requested to receive Morning Inspiration, the need to shift my focus became clear. Morning Inspiration was no longer solely directed at women going through illness. Grieving hearts, moments filled with uncertainty, self-discovery, and the love of awareness also started finding their way into my morning inspirations.

The rewards of expanding my circle of daily inspirations were magnificent, but sometimes it was challenging to sustain. There were days when my thoughts, words, and inspiration seemed hidden between the trees of my soul's forest. But knowing that even one person relied on Morning Inspiration for a feel-good moment was reason enough to continue searching the many trails of my inner forest.

Five days a week, I uncovered treasures of awareness and shared them with people across the globe. I loved the responses and relationships that developed, feeling privileged by each one.

Stories of challenge and triumph continued to leave me in awe. But mostly I remained in awe of the human spirit.

Morning Inspiration and I would go through many transformations over the next eleven years. I learned to slow the pace of my moments, giving more room for gratitude and mindfulness. I was introduced to the loving world of grandparenthood, one like no other. My passion for writing became deeper and clearer. My words found a home, though more often in the poetic realm than in stories. I no longer felt committed to writing five days a week, adapting a more spontaneous way of creating.

Then, a newly adopted hobby, photography, became an important partner to Morning Inspiration, offering an additional place of inspiration, both for me and the reader.

Over the years, many members of the Morning Inspiration family would ask, "Why don't you put your Morning Inspirations in a book?" I would softly push the idea aside, relying on excuses of trepidation and childhood reservations. The seeds were being sowed, but it would take COVID lockdown to germinate the vision of a book. Time no longer accepted my justifications for putting off publishing. My "now" became even more precious. I knew that going through 3,687 emails would take time and discipline.

COVID offered me the time, and my love for this work granted the discipline.

As I went through years of my heart's messages, I tried to choose those that continued to awaken my spirit as if I were writing them for the first time.

All the while, I was imagining you, the reader, in your own unique way, discovering the words of these messages, words that have reached so many beautiful souls around the world.

So I sat down and tasked myself with going through all my past inspirational emails—culling the ones that spoke most deeply from my soul, seeming to capture the stories and moments and heart messages that were dearest to me and my readers. It wasn't easy, and yet it was a work of love.

This is how *A Heart's Landscape* was born.

Come sit and rest for a while.
Read a word, a paragraph, or a sentence.
There is no correct order or right pace.
Let the book stay open or closed.
No instructions or tasks.
This is your time, a time to nourish your soul, your heart.
A hand when yours needs holding.
An ear when your laughter craves to be heard.
A place of rest, a place of calm.
A place of encouragement and inspiration.
A place for you, for all of you.

Welcome to this world of heart messages; what
a privilege it is to have you here.
Come sit and rest for a while.

A HEART'S LANDSCAPE

Imagine you are standing in the ocean as you notice in
the distance a beautiful wave coming your way.

The white foam slowly getting higher and bubblier,
the sounds of the wave singing louder.

The cool, refreshing sea is about to meet up with you.

The anticipation itself can be captivating!

It is in your power to choose to immerse yourself fully in the wave,
to ride above it with caution, or to quickly move away from it.

Similar are your choices and power when you meet
up with changes on your personal journey.

You can fully embrace the changes with excitement, diving into
the refreshing and purifying happenings they may bring you.

You can choose to acknowledge their presence and
gracefully allow them to be part of your path.

Or you may also decide to ignore the changes
before you and not get "wet."

The next time you see the wave coming, be aware of your choices.

3

Many years ago, a wise teacher taught me that
each day I should practice a smile.

For no reason and with no expectation.

"Soon you will find your heart and soul smiling
with no effort," he explained.

I recall setting out a moment each day to
stop what I was doing and smile.

Slowly, infinite reasons for a smile embraced me.

I continue to practice this, not daily, but as often as I can.

Gift yourself a moment to smile for no reason;
the reasons may grow and grow.

Before Waze was a thing, we had maps.

While traveling somewhere unknown, we traced
the map, as a guide to our destination.

At times demanding a stop off the road, in order to find our way.

Sometimes, while stopping off the road, I would
notice something breathtaking;

Losing my way allowed me to find new places
I would have never arrived at.

Our moments may lead us to the unfamiliar,
causing confusion for our inner map.

We may be lost just for a bit; we may need to
stop in order to find a new way.

While tracing your new inner map, bring your awareness
to something beautiful you have never noticed.

Trust the map reader in you; you will find the right road.

The only bull story I had ever heard was about Ferdinand.

My oldest daughter and I would snuggle in bed, night after night, and I would read her the story of a sweet bull who chose to smell flowers rather than fight in the bullring.

She adored this story; perhaps it was that she herself was not much of a fighter but rather a flower lover.

Perhaps it was the repletion, the calmness of ritual.

One day she took the book from my hand and started reading it to me.

I remember that moment well; a bit of innocence left the universe.

My daughter was taking a few more steps without me.

Even so, I hoped my arms would forever remain a place of calm and safety.

6

I also recall thinking that would probably be my last bull story.

Many years later, by chance, another bull story came my way; for some reason, it caught my eye.

I learned there is a place in the bullring where the bull feels safe.

If he is able to reach this spot, he can gather
his strength and stop running.

Fear no longer possesses him.

I inquired into the bull's safe place and found it is called a *querencia*.

Today, my daughter is a mother of three wonderful children.

They lie safely in her arms in their querencia.

You have a querencia as well.

A place where strength is gathered and courage is found.

Close your eyes and feel your querencia wrap its arms around you!

Yesterday, a good friend shared her love for the sound of rain.

Presenting my heart with a new awareness.

Curiously waiting with different listening for the next rainfall.

Nature answered my inquisitiveness!

Heavy rain, proclaiming her greatness, greeted me this morning.

Nurturing nature's children with the gifts of water.

Creating swishy puddles to jump in.

Washing away the remnant dust of prior heat-wave days.

Giving space to the tears from above.

Knocking rapidly on my window, awakening my attentiveness.

Listening with a newness to the beat of my heart.

8

He sits on a corner close to a traffic light.

His legs are crossed, and a blue blanket covers him.

The tip of his hood disguises any hint of a face.

An arched body trying desperately to warm itself.

I pass by that corner a few times a week.

The picture never changes.

"Would you like some hot coffee?" I always ask.

He lifts his head slightly, gifts a toothless smile, and responds. "I loved it yesterday and the time before and the time before that. I think I will love it today as well."

Our hands touch, and he holds on for a second, taking the coffee and slowly returning to be one with his curving body.

Today, when you witness tough, offer a loving hand.

The gift of the moment will keep on giving.

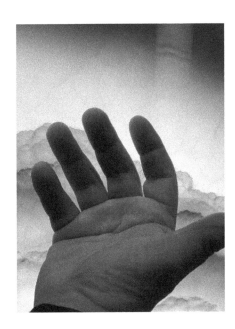

9

Listen to what I have to say.

Hear me; hear what my heart is voicing.

There is no need to coach, or ask questions.

Hold my hand, hug me, but please don't use words.

Look into my eyes and let your unconditional
compassion hold my soul.

Listen to what I have to say.

Be with me; just be with me.

Time is funny like that.

It can hold our soul in stillness or let it drift without noticing.

It can remind us of what was and what is.

It can be a book filled with infinite stories.

It can sit in the palm of our being, shaped
with the guidance of our spirit.

Time can be yours, this moment, the next, and the next.

Time is funny like that.

My granddaughter and I spent some alone time yesterday.

I learn some of my most important lessons this way.

We laughed, danced, and spoke conversations of the heart.

I held a shofar (the horn that is blown over the
days of awe in synagogues) in my hand.

Her mother, my daughter, had brought this home many years ago.

Up until yesterday, I had not experienced the strong
importance of its presence in my home.

My granddaughter and I examined it together, feeling
the softness, the interesting swiveling shape, and
the two different openings on each end.

One side, the one you blow into, is narrow; the other
side, the one the sound exits from, is wider.

"There is a narrow place, but at the end, there is a wider one," I
started to explain, hoping to share with her that from every narrow
place, there is a wide range of opportunities and possibilities.

Yet, my sweet and so-very-honest granddaughter replied, "*Savta*
['Grandma' in Hebrew], when you look through this small hole, it's
dark, but if you look through to the other side, there is so much light!"

I smiled and held her close.

What a wonderful reminder!

From every dark place, there is always a way to see the light.

For many years, I have had a dress in my closet.

It floats, beautifully pressed on a satin hanger.

I purchased it in a store that was beyond my budget at the time.

Thinking and hoping I would have a special day to wear it.

Special moments came and went, and I never thought
the day was special enough for the dress.

A number of years ago, that extraordinary day
with many special moments had arrived.

14

I couldn't wait to slip into my beautiful blue dress!

However, the dress no longer fit; parts were
too big and others too small.

I would not be able to enjoy the "dress moment"
I had anticipated for so long.

Sometimes we wait for the best moment, but
every day there are best moments.

Every day has a treasure; every day has special moments.

The dress still hangs in my closet as a reminder to be in the
special of today and not wait for what tomorrow will bring.

I may just slip into that dress today, twirl
around, and enjoy a special moment.

Through the hallways of life, the tunnels of time, I have
visited the many rooms in my heart's house.

I have witnessed a beautifully decorated room,
colors galore, glorious joy in every corner.

I have found myself in a room filled with
echoes of pain, hurt, and grief.

I have spent much time in a room embodied with love and kindness.

I have celebrated in a room surrounded by blessings and gratitude.

I have patiently resided in a room of peacefulness and calm.

I have sat in a room while facing restraints of the past.

I have held hands in a room overflowing with courage and bravery.

The windows in each room have offered me views.

Some I have kept ingrained in the walls of
my heart; others I have set free.

Owning the privilege to choose the contents
and decor I wish to maintain.

Through the hallways of life and the tunnels of time, I
have visited the many rooms in my heart's house.

Today, own your privilege to choose the contents
and decor of the rooms in your heart's house.

I have been working on a project for the last year and half in helping to bridge communities, and bridge people who stem from various beliefs.

I have learned so much from these extraordinary humans.

I have witnessed the ability of humankind to discover acceptance, to let go of prior judgments, to embrace another with an open heart and clear vision.

I believe that when we can become more accepting of our own humanness and limitations, we can become more accepting of others' humanity and limitations.

As time went on, I witnessed how this true self-acceptance enabled people to see one another for their uniqueness.

They were able to discover the holiness, the sacred that each one of them embodied.

Perhaps the more wholly they saw each other, the more holy they became.

The ripple effects are enormous; the more we become integrated, the more we are able to observe the integrity of this life.

Honor your humanity, your wholeness, your holiness, and allow your heart to discover the amazing uniqueness of others.

I stepped outside and watched the picture for a moment.

I watched the people I love dearly just be.

They laughed, discussed with great passion, enjoyed a shared serenity.

A sense of compassion and unconditional love was present.

I placed this picture in the photo album of my soul.

Forever there to view.

Take a moment and step out of the picture.

Place the beauty of what you see in the photo album of your soul.

A few days ago, I spent time in a pool with
my seven-year-old granddaughter.

We danced, sang, and embraced silliness.

However, the fear of swimming filled small spaces surrounding her.

I have seen her swim; the knowledge exists.

As we headed to the deep end, a tense silence emerged.

"I need to be near the wall," she shared.

Together we swam side by side as we approached her safe space.

Her strenuous movements, filled with struggle, exhausting her.

At that moment, I recalled the importance of floating.

When we stop struggling, we float.

Floating requires letting go, trusting that the
water beneath us can hold us, lift us!

So we floated, side by side, our fingers occasionally touching.

Sounds of a silent calm emerged.

We practiced floating for a while; we practiced relaxing her fear.

In the end, there is no real way to prepare for
letting go other than to just let go!

"I am ready to swim now," her sweet voice proclaimed.

Facing the deep water with newly restored strength.

I hope her sense of floating, of letting go, will
remain in her heart's memory.

Take a break from your struggles and float.

Let your being be lifted and held.

I was sure we had fixed all the holes and secured a flood-free basement.

Alas, the force of water found a new way to
engage us in a familiar cleanup.

The water vac was brought out; boxes and
equipment found a new height.

The cause was discovered, problem solved.

In the midst of reorganizing, I came across a box in a far-off corner.

I brought it to a dry area, sealed, with no description.

The surroundings were already conditioned as new,
leaving time for my hands to let curiosity lead them.

With excitement I removed the tape as energy of the past emerged.

As I stooped over the brown cardboard box,
my fingers touched what once was.

Letters written by those who were and who are no longer, handmade
cards decorated with flowers for each childhood birthday of mine.

This time I read them with a new attentiveness, one
that housed a forgiving and healing heart.

I welcomed my unexpected findings, some
with tears, some with laughter.

Mostly with a new heart view.

Invite a new heart view into your moment.

It is amazing what the heart can see with a new pair of glasses.

Take the gentle path; meet up with what comforts you.

During my morning stretches, I looked up at the clouds.

I can't remember the last time I took such an attentive look at them.

The familiar fluffiness, white softness, and
surrounding blue were all there.

As my body attempted to reach new lengths, I saw
the beauty of unity and individualism.

For each cloud that moved, it found a bigger
cloud or group to attach to.

Releasing another with a slow and gentle movement.

The single cloud drifting for a short while until
it found a new group of clouds to join.

Like the clouds, we all need to find time to
unite, and time to be by ourselves.

Today, find a gentle moment to balance your
unity and your individualism.

Home Economics class was a place where girls
learned to cook, sew, knit, or crochet.

Shop was where the boys studied carpentry and mechanics.

Gender was a thing.

My father, the son of a tailor, knew how to sew.

He made the clothes for his first granddaughter's doll.

He also was a carpenter, a talented handyman.

He built his first granddaughter the cradle she slept in.

His green thumb created beautiful gardens.

Perhaps planting the seed in my heart space,

as well as my mind space, that I could do both.

I haven't built a cradle, yet I can comfortably be handy when needed.

I never sewed doll clothes; however, I have just
finished crocheting my eighth blanket.

My hands have created numerous gardens.

Restricting our world of creating eliminates joyous moments.

You are the master of your creativity, in
whatever direction your heart chooses.

I have had many lessons of courage in my life.

With each lesson, I have received homework.

Some I have completed, and others are still a work in progress.

Courage has offered me the ability to reveal my shortcomings.

To embrace vulnerability.

Courage has visited when I least expected it,
holding my hand as I took the next step.

My teachers have been people I know closely,
others I have never spoken with.

In the classroom of my soul, courage has
taught me to harvest my failures.

Self-judgment has a much harder time entering my moments.

Be aware of the lessons courage has for you as
you attend the classroom of your soul.

I have always had plants living in my home.

Most of my plants have been with me for
twenty years, some even longer.

They are mostly green; at different seasons,
colorful leaves and flowers decorate them.

They are a visual reminder of growth, a living force.

I make sure to feed them the water they need, to cut back the
overgrown stems that seem to reach unreachable places.

Their fresh verdant color adding a glow around my home.

When we feed our soul, just as I feed my plants water,
growth of the heart, spirit, and mind follow.

Your entire being glows.

Listen for the sound of rain.

On a crowded subway in midday, I sat quietly.

My mind was taking a rest as I knew my day was a busy one.

I offered my seat to an older woman.

She turned to me and asked, "Do I look that old? Do I look tired?"

She sat down comfortably as her pink coat wrapped her slender body.

I moved a bit closer to her and responded, "No,
not at all. You're quite beautiful!"

"Is it my hair or my coat?"

I looked at her and smiled. "Neither. Actually, it's
your smile that is filled with beauty."

Her voice was soft as she continued to talk with me.

I found myself bending down, looking straight into
her eyes that seemed to be filled with life.

"All you need is a good sense of humor to have a
good life," her voice said with sparks of joy.

I nodded and responded, "Absolutely."

"Have a happy day," I told her, and turned to the subway door.

She gently touched my shoulder and said,
    "You, you have everything happy."

I thanked her as I was about to exit, when she shouted
    in her gentle voice, "Wait! Miss, have a happy life!"

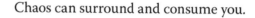

Chaos can surround and consume you.

As a client once described to me, "When chaos becomes too great, I feel as if I were in my kitchen junk drawer, where nothing can be found."

One thing that can never be lost in the chaos is the soft center of your heart.

The place that finds your courage, the place that finds your unlimited love and compassion.

The place that finds your willingness to take the risk.

The place that finds your gratitude for the simplest of joys.

The place that allows your eyes to listen and believe in what they cannot see.

When you are connected to your heart, you can hear the voice that rises above the chaos: *I will be all right.*

Be all right.

When disarray and messiness find you, listen to the soft center of your heartbeat!

34

We passed each other from a distance.

Her mask was a light blue; mine was a denim color.

Our hands covered in gloves, we quickly
pushed our carts while looking away.

A brief moment held us.

We turned our heads toward each other.

I couldn't see her smile under her mask, but I felt mine.

A moment of connection, her eyes smiled back.

We stood still for a brief second.

Taking in the goodness that filled the energy around us.

Goodness never gets lost.

35

It lives within us, waiting only for an invitation to show its beauty.

One moment of kindness.

Quietly touching one heart.

Whose heart then touches another.

Reaching out to infinite ends.

One moment of kindness, a gift to others, a gift to you.

There is something exceptionally relaxing about planning not to plan!

Knowing that the plan is secondary, and the present
moment is at the forefront, offers a breeze of calmness.

We arrange so much of our day; taking part
in an unplanned plan can be a treat.

Gifting yourself with the unknown and hidden joys a moment holds.

Choose some time today to be in the unplanned.

One morning, afternoon, or evening, you just get it!

The freedom of realization occurs.

What is of importance and what is not.

You learn the liberty to care less about what others think
of you and more about what you think of yourself.

You just get it!

Your entire being can feel how far you have come.

You remember when things were filled with such confusion and mess.

And you thought you would stay in it forever.

And then you smile; your heart smiles; your soul smiles.

In that moment, you are truly proud of yourself, and
the person you so passionately fought to be.

It just clicks!

I was having dinner with my adorable granddaughter when once again her honesty brought such wisdom to the room.

My daughter: "I am explaining it to you. Are you listening?"

A moment of silence.

My granddaughter: "No!"

Letting someone know you are not available to listen at a particular moment is a gift both to them and to yourself.

Many words filled with heartfelt meaning are lost in the wind that blows between a speaker and an unavailable listener.

Listen when your heart is available, and when it's not, share the fact with gentle honesty.

Pay attention to the availability your heart has to listen.

May your moments of stillness
reveal the courage you are.

The snow falling down this morning is soft.

It gently lands with no sense of force but rather a quiet greeting.

Changing nature's March scene to a powdered-sugar one.

Changes need not be made with severity.

When change is invited with a light softness,
a calming serenity greets it.

Allowing for its purpose to be known.

Make room in your heart for all of you.

The loving, kind, doubting, fearful you.

The angry, caring, silly you.

The messy, daring, relaxed you.

The brave, sad, adorable you.

Make room in your heart for all of you.

The forgiving, wise, impatient you.

Make room in your heart for you, all of you.

Don't tell me it will be fine.

Don't tell me it will all work out.

Just sit here beside me and hold my hand.

For in your grasp, I find the courage and bravery
to make my next moment a good one.

One day, after she had suffered an unfathomable loss,
she sat silently in a room filled with people.

They came to her with smiles, asking questions,
saying words that she could not process.

Every now and then a familiar face appeared, but
she could not recall why they were there.

A wave of enormous exhaustion came over her, her
soul trying hard to swim in the sea of trauma.

She felt someone take her hand, transmitting the calm that
helped her spirit find the courage and strength it needed.

Reminding her being that compassion does not
need the right words to be present.

Knowing she had been seen for the person she is, not as the
trauma she had faced, was her power, her endurance.

Today, let someone know they have been seen.

45

The heat was strong.

The air felt dry and heavy.

An early-morning drive, I saw sand and thirsty plants.

Just as I was convinced that the heat had put the beauty
of northern Israel on hold, suddenly color appeared.

Pink blossoms, and red, yellow, and white flowers
covered the bushes on both sides of the road.

Excitement awakened my soul as if I had
seen colors for the very first time.

I knew my eyes had met up with this landscape before.

I had driven this road at this time of year hundreds
of times before, but I let this time be different!

Letting yourself see something beautiful you have seen many times
before, as if it were for the very first time, is a glorious treasure.

Take a stroll down a road you have walked before
and rediscover the beauty it offers.

His movements are slow and gentle.

His eyes continue to light up the room.

So bravely he shares his laughter.

Consciously meeting my eyes.

Making sure I know he is still the same person
I have known for so many years.

We laugh and laugh some more.

Laughter—true, honest laughter—brings a moment of healing.

Courage is the ability to invite laughter when sinking
into cloudy moments seems so much easier.

May your moments find the compassion
and love that laughter can offer.

47

Today, find the woman within you.

When you find her, you will know it.

Today, find the woman within you.

When you go after your heart's desires and beliefs,
you will know that you heard her voice.

Today, find the woman within you.

You need her to guide you.

When your compassion and humility grow,
you will know her presence.

She will softly whisper your beauty, your
ability to embrace the unknown.

Today, find the woman within you.

She will tell you all you have forgotten.

Reminding you to be loyal to yourself, to your spirit.

I try to stretch every morning.

It enables a gentle flow of energy that welcomes a bit more flexibility.

Our body as well as our heart and mind
can enjoy the gift of suppleness.

Flexibility gifts us with the capacity to bend without
breaking, invite change where needed.

A flexible mind allows us to take advantage of
opportunities that so softly wait to be discovered.

Let the world continue to surprise and delight you.

Be flexible, welcoming the unexpected.

My rosebushes are once again filled with healthy green leaves and tiny buds waiting to bloom.

They seem to get stronger each year.

It amazes me how they survive the winter.

They practically are bare by the time winter exits.

I see them for what they are.

No blooming colors or outstanding fragrances.

Bare branches, some wounded, some barely hanging on.

They just are!

Their trust in nature, their roots and soil that
hold them, is quite awe-inspiring.

Somehow, they come through the various storms,
stronger and more beautiful than before.

They make room for their beautiful flowers.

We have all gone through storms, and somehow
our flowers continue to blossom!

Know there is always room for more of your flowers to appear!

Children have the ability to be one with their imagination.

They have the creative freedom that at times we as adults don't.

My grandchildren played a softball game
yesterday with no balls and no bats.

Never allowing their imagination to be hindered;
rather, the opposite, to be nurtured.

Imagination is a beautiful tool of guidance.

Helping us discover the magnificent that
can translate into our moments.

Today, allow your imagination to bring something into existence.

Who knows, you too could be part of a softball game!

On a small table in front of my window sits a healthy plant in a basket.

Every now and then, it produces a small yellow rose.

This morning, it appeared quite unannounced,
quietly making a statement.

There is also an ice storm outside, and I was gifted a rest day midweek.

The contrast of this springlike yellow flower looking out
at the dark gray sky was my awareness moment.

A burst of color can be found at the most unexpected
time, a stepping-stone as we wait out the storm.

Today, be aware of the unexpected color in your moments.

I looked out my window this morning, and
to my surprise there was a gift!

In the darkish early-morning hour an
extraordinary view was before me.

A sunrise!

Slowly peeping up with a bright yet soft hello.

For that moment, I was in awe.

This sunrise had touched and awakened me in a new way.

I stood still, silent and observant.

Awe is the way our soul expresses wonder.

Invite awe into your moments!

I sent my youngest daughter off to her senior
year of college this morning.

Reminding my soul that it is time to let go, once again, a little bit more.

As a mom, I have learned that with each "letting go,"
I give both myself and my daughters a gift.

A gift of stronger wings to fly, for both of us.

Setting out to discover more about ourselves and
what awaits us in the moments of our days.

Each step of "letting go" is often accompanied
by a hesitant, quiet breath.

A breath that somehow enables my arms to open even wider.

Ready to receive the opportunities that
unexpectedly will come my way.

Try taking a "letting go" breath.

Perhaps, it will open your heart to new and exciting discoveries.

The storm Irene brought much anxiety and damage to many.

Listening to the heavy rains, the swaying of
angry winds, jolting thunder and lightning, was a
reminder that so much is out of our control.

Walking outside after the storm, I was met
by many fallen trees and branches.

Evidence that things had changed.

No longer were nature's children standing as they had the previous day.

However, this morning the sun is shining; the air
is fresh; quiet sounds of birds welcome me.

A new day, a new beginning.

Signs of Irene are slowly disappearing.

Storms come into our lives; many of them are not in our control.

With heart awareness, rays of sunshine may find our spirit.

I watched the sun rise this morning.

Water, a bridge, floating clouds, all in my view.

A bright sun made my heart jump with
anticipation, excitement, and curiosity,

in awe of what the day's moments would bring.

A day is made up of many moments.

Each moment has the potential to make your soul smile.

Catch a look at your own beautiful sunrise!

You may be in awe of the exquisiteness you find.

This week I was incredibly blessed with the gift of
holding my month-old grandson in my arms daily.

He is a gentle soul and seems to be extremely
content with the gift and miracle of his life.

As infants go, finding a position that comforts them can be a challenge.

My grandson prefers to be held in a way that
his eyes can meet mine at close range.

His big blue eyes invite my eyes to moments of
silence that speak the language of my heart.

The intimacy you share with someone when you look into the
soul of their eyes rewards your being with unbounded joy.

When was the last time you looked someone
straight into the depth of their eyes?

Maybe today arrange a meeting between
your eyes and the eyes of another.

*There is always a blessing
in the air; we just need
to breathe it in.*

My middle daughter is getting married in two weeks,
and my heart is filled with motherly emotions.

I have always found music to help clear the pathways to my heart.

The words, the tunes, the combination of both.

Awakening the faith, hope, and trust my soul
desires to help me on this new journey.

Listening to music invites my heart to sing. I sing with
joy; I sing with memories; I sing with excitement.

Perhaps, most of all, I sing with love for my little girl.

Today, surround yourself with music; invite your heart to sing.

I was preparing a small package for a woman
awaiting to enter the hospital for treatment.

I thought I knew exactly what I was looking for, a
prayer I have shared with many women.

A power much larger than I am suggested perhaps
I should read something else first.

Searching through a pile of inspirational notes, I came across
words of wisdom, words of healing, words of blessing.

Words that were written by a woman I had met on a spiritual
retreat, who had an amazing, sacred energy about her.

I read the words out loud, slowly, making sure my
heart could hear the story each word had to tell.

The message penetrated my soul, demanding
from me to repeat these profound words.

I found myself singing them, singing from my heart,
as small tears trickled down my cheeks.

I welcomed the burst of emotional energy as I slowly ended "my song."
Unforeseen to me, my spirit needed its own moment of healing.

Sometimes the heart and soul are touched by an unexpected source.
Today, welcome the messages that come your way.

Be patient with yourself.

Seeds don't grow or blossom in a day.

Growth and change are a process.

Each stage is of great importance; each stage counts!

Just as each seasonal cycle brings about change and growth to nature,

the cycles and seasons within our soul bring
about change and growth to our being.

Be patient with yourself.

Nourish the seeds in your soul; trust your process of growth!

Be patient with yourself.

Sometimes the sun hides.

One can sense the sun, feel its presence,
even though it is not to be seen.

The sky gives off a slightly gray feeling.

The sun is not shining, but rather patiently waiting to appear.

It reminds us every now and then that it exists
by quietly peeking through the clouds.

Perhaps waiting for the appropriate moment, for an invitation.

As is the sun in your moments.

At times hiding, at times peeking, and at times shining brightly.

But always there for you to invite.

Today, find a moment to invite your sun to shine.

One moment of enthusiasm

provides your being with a burst of heartfelt joy!

One moment of enthusiasm awakens your soul with self-made caffeine.

Once a day, pause and gift yourself a moment of enthusiasm.

During my hike yesterday, I noticed a beautiful yellow butterfly.

She sat herself in complete stillness for a short
moment or two on a perfectly shaped rock.

Her wings not giving way to the slightest fluttering.

And then, with no warning, she took off.

Flying ever so elegantly into the beautiful skies.

Reminding me of the many butterfly moments I have experienced.

Being in my stillness in preparation as I flew off into the unknown.

There is a beauty and strength like no other that stillness provides.

As your wings are able to fly, to take that risk into the
unknown, to step out of your comfort zone, be in stillness.

When have you experienced a butterfly moment?

Things to do:

Be in a moment of silence.

Feel the beauty of your heart beating.

Laugh more.

Give of your heart generously.

Express yourself creatively.

Make time to be with yourself.

Make time to be with others.

Move your body.

Invite your spirituality into your moments.

Empty them from unneeded stress.

I have adopted the custom of wishing people a "Happy Day" as I exit a store or bid farewell to someone.

Never quite knowing what the reaction to follow will be.

This practice allows for my heart to be in the presence of positive energy for that very moment.

Yesterday, as I left a shop, I wished a young woman: "Happy Day."

Her reaction is still with me today.

"Wow, no one has ever wished me that. I can't wait to pass that message on. Thank you for reminding me that happiness is there for me," she replied, barely catching her breath with excitement.

Share the power of positive energy, a gift to your being as well as to someone else's.

Spring is starting to become obvious here in the Northeast.

The trees are showing off their buds, and bulbs
are proudly sharing their colorful flowers.

Birds are everywhere, singing their tunes, happily greeting each other.

That is nature's spring.

Then there is "my spring."

I have always adopted spring as a time to clear away
the old and make room for the new growth.

A time to make a new order in my home as well as in my heart.

With each drawer or closet I clean out and organize,
I have cleared yet another soul drawer.

Unblocked a doorway to my heart, opened
a different window to my spirit.

The freshness of "my spring" enters my home; all
that is no longer needed slowly leaves.

The beauty of newness begins to surround me.

Today, do a bit of your own "spring cleaning."

73

The sound of the waves.

The view of the ocean and sky meeting.

The gentle wind and warm sun together stroking my face.

The sun dusting my toes.

This is my place of peace.

Where my mind, body, and soul rest as one.

Not always able to arrive there physically, I have taught
my breath to take me there as I close my eyes.

May your place of peace be with you wherever you are.

I have been discovering new corners in my home.

I have lived here for over twenty-five years.

I remember the first time I met this house.

The door entrance held hopes, dreams, fears, and much joy.

Many of those dreams changed shapes; some hopes
were met; others silently disappeared.

Fears left through the back door; others still
visit when windows are left open.

At times, tears wrapped themselves around my soul.

However, more than anything, joy decorated
the windows, walls, and floors.

Joy was often heard through the speakers of our hearts in this house.

Perhaps, I took this house for granted.

I never expected a pandemic to give me the opportunity
to once again experience the wonders of my home.

Reconnect with the corners of your home and the comfort it offers.

Of late, my delicious grandchildren have been putting on shows.

They dance and sing with no restrictions.

They move and share their tune with no
concern for how well they are doing.

Somewhere along the way, we seem to lose that freedom.

We sit out more dances, and quiet our song.

Concerning ourselves with what others may see.

Don't sit your moments out; don't lose touch
with your special and beautiful rhythm.

Know that your liveliness thrives on your
song, your dance, your rhythm.

When your car's maintenance light comes on,
you know it's time to take care of it.

You drive to a car-repair shop.

Your soul also needs maintenance.

However, many times we seem to ignore the light
indicating so, blinking in front of us.

Believing that we can keep going, doing what we have to.

Why is it that we hurry to tend to our car's needs
and not to our very own soul's needs?

Your soul deserves to be maintained at the
most joyful and serene level.

What does your soul need to "work well"?

What energizes it, nurtures it, allows it to be the best it can be?

Be aware of your soul's maintenance light.

Is it blinking?

I took a walk yesterday along a small beach not far from me.

I was dropping my granddaughter off at an art class
nearby and decided to visit the serene place.

As I entered the park, I was greeted by numerous
people, walkers and strollers like myself.

Each greeting was accompanied by a warm smile, a blessing
for a good day, and a burst of beautiful energy.

As I got closer to the water, I sat on a bench in stillness.

Listening to the birds, the quiet water, and
the footsteps of those walking by.

On a nearby bench, an older couple sat cuddled together,
silently staring into the gentleness of the view.

I was reminded of the beauty in my own backyard.

Discover the beauty in your own backyard; it is a gift.

A number of years ago, I had a lecture appointment.

As I was about to enter the hall, I realized I
needed a quick run to the bathroom.

Concerned that I would be late to my introduction, I
rushed back and forth, barely making it on time.

I knew my beginning words would be the ones
to open the hearts in the room.

However, there were chuckles coming from
different corners of the room.

People were desperately trying to hide their laughter.

I found the courage to look out into the room filled with over one
hundred people and asked to be part of the entertaining laughter.

A sweet seventy-something woman came up
to me and kindly pointed to my rear!

I had been aware of a breeze, but didn't know from where.

My dress had gotten caught up in my leggings, and
my rear was practically exposed to all.

I looked to the room as I gently covered
what no longer needed to be seen.

The audience was waiting to see what I
would do with this odd moment.

I laughed, opening my lecture with a message.

When you can laugh at yourself, you can see how darling you are!

Even today, years later, I find myself laughing a good
laugh when I recall that November day.

Have a good laugh, a laugh at yourself!

I stood at my window and watched another tree become bare.

Naked and vulnerable, but firm and well rooted.

Storms may break her branches off, but her
roots are strong and grounded.

She knows where she stands; she knows who she is.

She knows that after the winter storms, she will have a chance
to bring forth new branches producing new green leaves.

The ground, the earth is her support.

She stays well connected.

Let your vulnerability lead you to your strength, support, and roots.

Time does not wait for us; handle it with heart attention.

On my first visit to the United States, thirty-seven years
ago, with my then new husband, I discovered a plant.

It was a cold December, with much snow on the ground, bare
branches, and hidden flowers that were left to the imagination.

Coming from a country where green and blooming colors still showed
their faces during the winter, I found that this plant caught my eye.

It sat in my mother-in-law's kitchen.

In a white basket by the window, long branches with soft
green leaves held the blooming pink flowers up proudly.

"How is it that during this very cold winter, this plant presents
such lush, beautiful pink flowers?" I innocently asked her.

She put her hand softly on my shoulder,
something she rarely did, and explained:

"In Europe during the worst of times, in the worst of moments, I
found faith. I found that I had a pink flower; I just needed to believe
in it. When I came to America after the war, I saw this plant and
was amazed like you at its choice to bloom with such an exciting
pink, even when the gray cold weather was so prominent."

In my home, next to a window, in a white basket sits that very
same plant, passed on to me from my mother-in-law.

It is December, and her pink flowers are blooming beautifully.

The ground is covered with much cold snow,
and the color gray fills the sky.

I am reminded how lucky we are to have that inner
pink flower, but it needs to be nurtured.

Water your inner pink flower.

Faith may help it blossom.

I did it again!

A number of days ago, I found myself dancing in my living room.

I was listening to music while I was cooking; as if a
"Play" button were pushed, I began to dance.

I twirled; I moved with fast steps; I shook parts of my
body that I had forgotten had talents of their own.

I danced.

There were no boundaries between me and the walls of
the room, the floor beneath me, or the trees outside.

I tasted the joy of belonging to the very force of the universe.

As I continue to cultivate ways of celebrating
joy in my moments, I learn.

I learn to enjoy the full variety of pleasures
the moments of my day hold,

even when hardships may appear.

Making it possible for joy to find me at the most unexpected moments.

Find a moment to let go of the boundaries that
keep joy from entering your moment.

Slow down enough to look around.

Slow down enough to understand how other people
feel, enough to be less quick to anger.

Slow down enough to appreciate more, enough to
love the people in your life with intent.

Slow down enough to enjoy your blessings,
enough to listen to the silence of others.

Slow down enough to open the door to your heart, enough to feel
the power in letting things in rather than keeping them out.

Slow down enough to welcome and offer forgiveness.

Slow down enough to invite change, enough to just be!

Walk with someone, and they may find the courage to run.

Look with them, and they may remember the beauty in seeing.

Hear with them, and in the quiet of your joint hearing,
they may discover the gift of listening.

Sing with them, and their heart will forever
understand the delight in rejoicing.

89

I had the wonderful fortune this week to reconnect with
a friend I haven't seen or spoken to in many years.

I have known her for forty years, and the time we spent
together introduced me to a new world of being.

I laugh out loud when I think of the many
funny moments we spent laughing.

I smile when I remember the many moments of unconditional
compassion that we shared for one another.

I shed a tear when my heart recalls the moments of pain
and sorrow that passed through our shared journey.

But mostly I feel gratitude for the wonderful world in
me I came to know because of our friendship.

Honor a friend and the world inside you they introduced you to.

90

Last night, at a holiday celebration, I danced, and danced some more.

Dozens of people danced with me, some I knew; others
became familiar faces as their hands held mine.

The music escorted all that were there into an
ongoing flow of soul-lifting energy.

I never looked at the time.

I loosened and dissolved my small separate
self into what was around me.

Awe guided me into incredible moments of happiness.

Allow yourself to dissolve into all that surrounds
you—invite awe to find your heart!

Joy never runs out, it is always waiting for you.

I was her meditation teacher; she wanted to dance.

The beat of her heart an open invitation to share in the dance of life.

The music of her soul constantly playing.

She wanted to dance.

Waiting for an invitation, she sat unable to hear her own music.

Not knowing that the best invitation would arrive.

All she had to do was listen to the beat of her
heart, to the music of her soul.

She wanted to dance.

We sat in silence, waiting for the first note to be heard.

Suddenly her feet began to tap; her body began to sway.

She found her dance; she heard her music; she
opened up her being to receive the invitation.

In a moment of silence, hear your music; let your dance lead the way.

I have returned home after being away for three weeks.

During my travels, my moments were met by people from
different countries, different ages, different genders.

However, I found myself enchanted not by the
differences but by the similarities.

When language was a barrier, it was their desire
to connect that opened my heart.

When their passion filled the air around us, it
brought my passion to a higher level.

When their eyes spoke of love, I found my hand
reaching out to hold and be held.

When gratitude for a moment of compassion couldn't be
translated into the spoken, my soul had filled a page of words.

Reminding me how the awareness of oneness brings people together.

Today bring focus to what you share with
others, not what differentiates you.

As I was traveling on the road, I noticed a colorful bus
with the most unusual sign on the back of it.

"Registration for the college for a happy heart is open."

I found myself smiling, digesting the message.

Ten minutes went by, and an additional bus with
the same sign passed me on my right.

I smiled and found myself laughing out loud;

I got the message loud and clear!

It was time to return to a place of laughter and joy!

I believe my moment needed that reminder.

Take a moment to learn about your very own college for a happy heart.

97

I recall helping a young woman change the
"decor" in her hospital room.

We redecorated, brought in "new" colors, added "works of art."

Her love for drawing became apparent, as art supplies were
suddenly available on the decorated tray that sat in front of her.

Bringing a colorful sense of joy into her room.

She had been hesitant to make any changes, to try something new.

Then came the moment when it hurt more to remain
with the same decor than to risk changing it.

An energy of accomplishment filled her hospital
room as a sense of calmness filled her soul.

Without taking that risk, one never can discover the beauty of change.

An encounter with one person for five minutes changed my day.

While I was waiting for my train, she ran up to me a bit frazzled.

"What side of the tracks do I wait on? This
is my first time on this train."

I assured her she was on the correct side; seeing she
was still not at ease, I started a conversation.

Never expecting what came after.

I learned how her faith had supported her in the hardest of times.

I listened as she shared her love for her
country of origin—the Philippines.

Her belief in humankind and trust, that the
value of peace lives in all our hearts.

Our train arrived; she waved goodbye and started walking to the train.

She turned toward me and said, "My name is Linda. It
was so nice meeting you; thank you for sharing."

I waved back and told her my name as I
thanked her for sharing as well.

I am not sure what I shared; perhaps it was a listening ear.

The optimistic energy she shared with me invited
my heart to smile for the rest of the day.

Pay attention to those you meet and those
who meet you—much can happen.

Walking toward the park yesterday, I noticed a pathway filled
with leaves that had fallen from the hovering trees.

The people walking by avoided the path, making
sure their shoes touched a leaf-free way.

I started following their walkway, but found myself thinking
about the wonderful crunch-like noise dry leaves make.

Knowing I was on a tight schedule, I tried to ignore
the colorful leaves swirling by my side.

However, "Playful Susan" wasn't willing to give up!

I slid over to the leaf-filled lane as my feet brought
the delightful crunchy sound to life.

My pace was fast; I had to be somewhere, yet I found myself pausing,

taking in the simple joy the crispy sounds had gifted me with.

101

The leaf lane came to an end, yet the moment
stayed with me throughout my day.

When "Playful You" calls, listen, stay with it, enjoy it, reconnect with it.

Being a savta (a grandmother) is a privilege
that fills my soul with gratitude.

A bond that has taken me back to the beauty only childhood can offer.

A trusting glance is the face of hope and faith.

The story that needs to be passed on.

Their little hands will be those that shape the world

with kindness, love, and compassion.

I think of that often.

Laughter shared with a child is the sound of loveliness.

As I hope my blanket of love continues to warm them,
I hope they make room for dreams to be born.

Be one with your now as if it were all that is, because it is!

Invite the teacher in your daughter to teach her daughter to shine.

Help her learn how to walk with her eyes fully open.

Encourage her to celebrate mystery rather than categorize.

Be her guide; let her be yours.

Be her partner.

Hear her insights, her shortcomings, her inspirations.

Listen to what lifts her soul.

Be with her.

Offer her an embrace filled with your time.

104

I hold him and am transformed.

The moment becomes timeless.

It is filled with the vastness of what life is all about.

His eyes hear my love as they look up, blue
and big, at the voice he hears.

Our hearts connect, and the miracle of life shows its face.

He will become one of my best teachers.

Just as each child and grandchild has done before him.

He will teach me to slow down and see the world through new eyes.

He will teach me to rediscover what I haven't seen in a long time.

He will teach me how to feel feelings I didn't know were there.

Like his mom, he will ascend into the world.

And I will do my best to hold her close as she sees him fly.

Today and tomorrow and the day after that,
connect with the miracle of life.

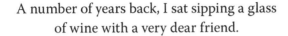

A number of years back, I sat sipping a glass
of wine with a very dear friend.

It was a beautiful sunny day.

We sat at a small table with an umbrella hovering over us.

His body weak, but his soul so very strong.

"What is it about today that makes you smile?" I asked him innocently.

He looked into my eyes and quietly answered.

"First of all, I get to be outside after many weeks of having
to stay inside; next, I am having a sip of wine with you.

"But most of all, it is that I have found another way to make today
matter. I think the hope that I will succeed lets me smile."

Words that have become a true guide for me.

Hope is moment by moment.

May you always find a moment of hope to give you the
strength you need to arrive at the next moment.

I have lived in a home that was a well-kept shed.

I have lived in a home that consisted of one room.

I have lived in a home that was shared by friends.

I have lived in a home filled with family.

I have lived in a home where fields of cotton formed my view.

I have lived in a home where pavement sidewalks greeted my eyes.

I have lived in a home where the large rooms and
space made for many solitary moments.

My inner sanctuary, the core of my being, is a home wherever I am.

Where I meet up with courage, breathe peace,
swim in love, and embrace my soul.

Wherever you find yourself, in whatever place your
home may be, your inner sanctuary awaits you.

106

Watching the water move with all its delicacy
and all its force is a sacred pause.

Listening to the sounds that surround me
with an open ear is a sacred pause.

Setting aside all that has to be done as I hold my
newest grandchild in my arms is a sacred pause.

Staring at the hovering sky just because is a sacred pause.

Sharing a smile with a new face is a sacred pause.

Breathing with intent is a sacred pause.

Writing these words is a sacred pause.

Coming into awareness is a sacred pause.

Each day the opportunities for a sacred pause
are infinite. What is your sacred pause?

When we take a sacred pause, we can feel life move through us.

A wish like hope is fragile.

It must be held with a gentle heart.

Caressed with nonjudgmental softness.

A wish like hope is fragile.

Housing it in the safety of your soul.

Protecting its unique beauty.

A wish like hope is fragile.

Passion and awareness are required to keep its golden light ignited.

Surrounding it with compassion and love for when it dims.

A wish like hope is fragile.

Yet has the strength and courage to carry you forward.

A wish like hope has the ability to be re-created over and over again.

Let the discovery of a wish hold your hand
and the presence of hope guide you.

When you are waiting, time is too slow.

When you are with fear, time changes.

When you grieve, time goes on too long.

When you are with delight, time is too short.

But, when you love, time is endless.

When I turned fifty, honesty presented itself so boldly.

Each word suggesting an awakened emotion.

Painting, dancing, raising orchids, all echoing the promptings
of a woman with the desire to learn, to follow her passions.

In my soft voice, I heard myself admitting it had been a long
time since I was able to hear my authentic longings.

Having spent many of my moments, caring for my family,
I hadn't heard the quiet whispers of my soul's desire.

Perhaps it's time to put yourself on your list of priorities
and be more loyal to your soul's desires.

Yesterday I shared the first dance with my grandson.

As I held him in my arms, his palm close to
mine, life seemed to stand still.

Both of us twirled around the room, with smiles bigger than our faces.

I chose the tune; he chose the accompanying sound effects.

What a perfect duet we created.

With each step that I took, I felt my heart melting with his.

From the side, my daughter observed, her
blue eyes smiling with glorious joy.

The three of us embraced by a great moment
that caught us off guard, unplanned.

One my daughter and I will most probably remember with much
more clarity than my sweet seven-month-old grandson.

I will continue to offer him my hand in dance, my hand
in life; for this opportunity I am forever grateful.

Allow yourself to get caught off guard, the unplanned and
spontaneous moments can be the most precious life has to offer.

One moment at a time, one challenge at a time,

one courageous soul, one hero.

That hero is you!

Nurture your heart with simplicity.

Fix your attention on the beautiful and the good.

Gentle moments, gentle rest.

Give your soul and body the gentle rest it needs.

The house was quiet.

In each room, loved ones were still dreaming
with the peacefulness of yesterday's joys.

I listened to the silence.

With each unheard noise, I heard the depth of gratitude speaking.

My heart overflowing with awareness of infinite blessings.

I witnessed a view of the moon bidding
goodbye as it made room for the sun.

The wonder of a new day, guided by the love of family and friends.

As my entire being was immersed in the serene
moment, the beauty of a tiny voice greeted me.

A pair of small hands reached out, wanting to be hugged.

I cannot think of a better way to begin this day.

Listen to the silence that is offered to you;
wondrous moments may follow.

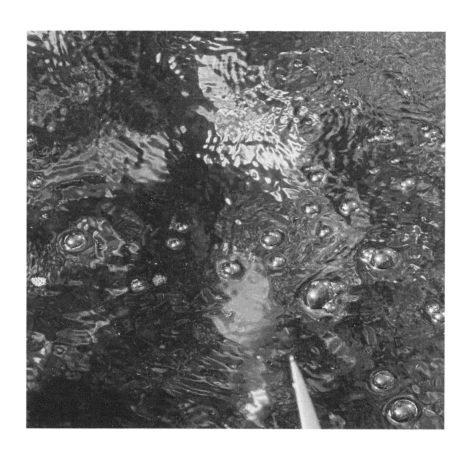

I have been going to a small dry-cleaning shop for twenty years.

When the store first opened, a young couple barely speaking
English welcomed me with an inviting, warm smile.

One that perhaps was the cause for my return time and time again.

114

Over the years, the sweet man's presence became scarce;
my visits to the store were with his gentle wife.

We developed a way to communicate, partly because her English
advanced and partly because my understanding of her improved.

We know a lot about each other.

Mostly about the joyous occasions and milestones in our lives.

We became parents of teenage children; we sent them off to college.

We shared the enjoyment of a white coat ceremony and
the excitement of our children's engagements.

We showed each other pictures of weddings and
glamour shots of our grandchildren.

With each sharing, there was a true sense of being in each other's joy.

I don't know her name.

I don't think she knows my first name.

However, we do know the true meaning of sharing joys.

The language of words need not be a barrier; to learn
someone's joys, just look into their eyes.

Put your hand on your heart; feel it beating.

That rhythm is a miracle.

The miracle of you!

Pause, breathe with intent.

Your courage and power are alive and well.

Trust the miracle of you.

It was late last night when I returned to my breath.

The breath that continues to remind me, peace can be found.

My peace, my calm.

Purposely and with intent giving focus to each inhale and exhale.

How I missed this tranquil quietude, hijacked
by the fast pace of my mind's moments.

The familiar warmth of a new breath filled
me, serenity flowing as it exited.

Thoughts come and go; some want to stay
longer than they are welcome.

The gift of a new breath may help them find the way out.

Acceptance.

Ups and downs, fast and slow.

Things move at a rapid pace, yet slowness surrounds us.

Information comes in, quickly changing the beat of our hearts.

Acceptance.

Cans and cannots, east and west.

Our compass not always easily at hand.

Yes and no, north and south.

Acceptance.

118

Reaching out to others with an invisible touch.

Caressing with faraway strokes.

Keeping my gratitude on a silver tray.

Creating a heart space.

For all that enters and all that leaves.

Acceptance.

Laughter can be wise.

It knows how to appear at the hardest of times.

We were sitting on the stairs, just the three of us.

We were each holding a glass of white wine.

As we sipped the cold, crisp wine, its cheap taste didn't seem to faze us.

The month was June, and the evening's summer
air felt wonderful on my face.

We were all mothers, and time to ourselves was an unknown entity.

It was late; our partners had taken the children for a walk.

The shifts of visitors had left.

Sounds of silence reminded us why we were there.

With no preparation, our giggling laughter appeared.

I can recall the release it offered, the momentary
solution to our mourning.

We had no answers; we had no tools, but we had laughter.

Laughter is wise; it knows when to appear.

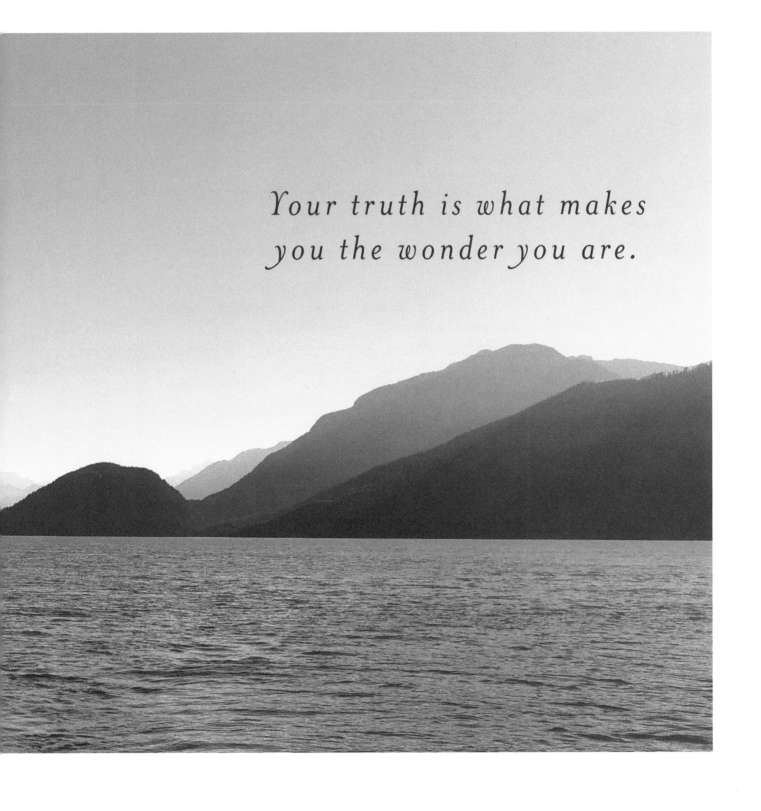

Your truth is what makes you the wonder you are.

Outside my window, wild sounds of wind and rain are heard.

Trees desperately trying to share their slowly
budding flowers swaying dramatically.

These days when the sunshine's healing is so
needed, I call upon my inner luminosity.

Sitting quietly in a familiar white chair in the corner of my bedroom.

A leather recliner that holds Winnie-the-Pooh softly in its lap.

I relaxed into my breath and stillness, the warmth
of memories flowing through me.

I have held each of my grandchildren in that chair.

I could smell their unique yet shared fragrance.

I inhaled their distant aroma, one of miracle, hope, love, and gratitude.

There is a magical perfume that grandchildren have.

Falling deeper into my moments, I could feel
their tiny hands grasping onto my finger.

Awakening a connection like no other.

In this comfy chair, I have sung lullabies to each of my grandchildren as their tiny souls slept so contentedly in my arms.

My heart longs to hold them close once again.

For today I call upon my inner luminosity, my stillness, my breath as I find a new way to feel their presence.

Call upon your inner luminosity to guide you.

Years ago I was privileged to teach young students that
there was no right or wrong way to creativity.

Through the use of different tools, they discovered personal creativity.

Bringing a shining light on the uniqueness each child owned.

One of the tools I used was a pair of puppets.

I remember making them, sewing, gluing in awe as
I watched them each take on a personality.

Their names were Gili and Yael, and they still reside in my home.

In the last month or so, they have come out to play once again.

Through the magic of screen time, my youngest
grandson has found two new friends.

Gili and Yael greet him with excitement and joy.

His bright blue eyes and delicious smile speak a language of awe.

Forty years old, my puppets continue to awaken the soul of creativity!

Reconnect with the creativity of yesterday; perhaps
it will be part of your creations today.

Jigsaw puzzles have become the new colorful
covering for my dining room table.

Each one presenting a different scene.

One thousand pieces in a bag, various colors and
shapes, that when put together, create a picture.

My youngest daughter reminded me that years ago I
taught her to start a puzzle from its corners.

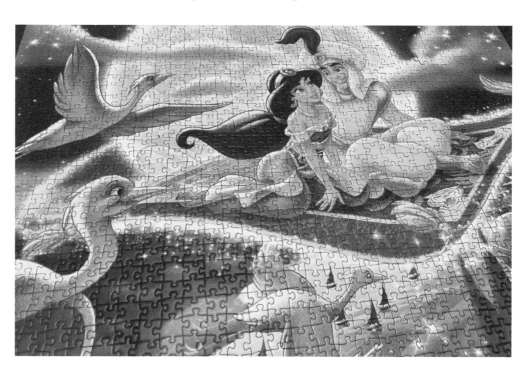

Separating the straight edges from the rest of the pieces.

Putting these puzzles together has sharpened my patience,
reminding my soul that solving puzzles takes time.

Some days my contribution to creating the
developing scene was larger than others.

Honoring the times I needed to take a break from being a puzzle solver.

Making way for my family members to contribute
their parts in helping a vivid picture appear.

Life's complexities can seem like a giant puzzle, making
it difficult to find a straight edge to begin with.

Honor your pace at finding the straight edges,
and the right fit for your pieces.

Make space for those who can offer you a contributing hand.

Your patience may present you with the most beautiful scene: *you*!

Today, may a piece to your puzzle become apparent.

I am fortunate to have an indoor room that overlooks my backyard.

Windows open, I can hear the sweet music of
birds, the calming flow of a fishpond.

A comfy, wide wicker chair has housed me for hours of meditation.

Making it a place where I can hear my heart's voice.

These past few months, I have learned to share this space.

Weekly, as well as spontaneously, I have found
a new form of intimacy with others.

Unable to meet at our homes, in restaurants, or across seas,
with Zoom's help, we found each other in this room.

Offering us a way to hug and hold hands when COVID-19 prevented it.

Opening my heart space to hear their voices in different ways.

To share mine, as sweet souls listened with a new attentiveness.

Although most of us have known each other for many
years, a refreshed sense of bond was discovered.

Renewing my gratitude for the precious
friendships and family I am blessed with.

Distance from those we love may not allow
us to hold a hand or embrace.

However, it may offer a new way for the
heart to speak as well as be heard.

Share your heart space; win over distance with those you love!

Today, take the plunge; travel with your heart to the unknown!

No need to pack a suitcase.

Grant your soul permission to take roads untraveled.

Let the gates of your heart open to others.

I watched their eyes as they spoke.

One had deep black eyes, the other brown.

Their faces appeared on two different screens.

Accents from the same homeland revealing the sounds of difference.

I could hear the pain from years ago alive in the words they spoke.

Yet it was their passion for hope, and determination
for good that were heard above all.

Over troubled waters a bridge was created.

What seemed inconceivable became a reality.

They took a risk, not knowing the outcome.

Choosing to take a first step rather than stand still.

Bring your attention to the possibility of
which a first step can take you.

Tears have no race, religion, or color.

Fear has no race, religion, or color.

The pain of the heart has no race, religion, or color.

Compassion and love have no race, religion, or color.

Today and every day, speak in kindness, give in kindness.

Today, and every day, receive in kindness.

Today, and every day, be in kindness.

Of late, I have been fortunate to enter the world
of make-believe with my grandchildren.

We have sailed on pirate ships, magical boats,
and been stranded on islands.

We have obtained magical powers as we fought off the virus.

We have expelled the bad and evil as we saved the good and loving.

We have proudly sung songs of victory as we
glanced through make-believe telescopes.

We have seen purple birds and yellow flying creatures.

At times, the innocence between reality and imagination
presented itself as we entered the waters of fantasy.

Once again entering the enchanting forest of childhood.

Invite the playful child in you to appear. You may be surprised
by the many adventurous moments that await you.

When your spirit is silent,
your moments go by unseen.

Plants have always been a part of my home.

Many have lived with me for well over twenty-five years;
others have joined my plant family more recently.

Their lavish green growth is a source of pride.

Some plants, producing little flowers now and then.

I tend to move them around when I sense they need a change.

Hoping it will keep them bright and sturdy.

Over the years I have become familiar with my flowering
plants, always amazed when a color appears in their pot.

About a month ago I moved a midsize green-
leafed plant to my kitchen sill.

Offering it a stage all to itself.

It lives in a turquoise ceramic planting pot.

Always seeming quite content with its branches
and calming green coloring.

However, this past weekend, it surprised
me with beautiful white flowers.

Changing my kitchen scenery!

Perhaps all that was needed was a bit of change.

Gathering sun from a different angle.

Like this plant, we all have unknown flowers, waiting to bloom.

Patiently eager to share the colors of our soul.

Welcome the sun from a different angle; your
radiant, colorful flowers may appear.

Park benches have hosted many.

Lovers, enjoying the romance of their newly found connection.

Lost souls, housing themselves in nature's shelter.

Young parents, catching quiet moments as
their little one sleeps in her stroller.

An elderly soul, sipping his coffee while reading his paper.

A runner, finding rest after her daily run.

Two siblings, excitedly strengthening their bond.

Girlfriends, catching up on stories that have yet to be told.

A park bench is a fond place of mine.

Offering me a seat of solitude or togetherness.

Awakening my curiosity with all the stories
of those who have come before me,

and those that will follow.

What awakens your curiosity?

Feel what is there.

Nothing to change.

Let the sensations of your moment arise.

Let it all be just as it is.

No need to limit your awareness.

Each sensation is its own experience.

Moment to moment.

Invite your heart to receive it all.

While on a boat, my body doesn't react well to
the dancing movement of the water.

Complicating my love for the ocean.

Never totally giving up, I have found keeping my eyes
focused on the view can soften the experience.

Yesterday, once again I attempted a boat ride.

The day was beautiful.

Blue calmness seemed promising as I boarded.

Surrounded by my three grandchildren, I relied on their
joyous presence to soften an uneasiness in my body.

Speed, passing boats, and exciting waves did not always cooperate.

We were heading to a small beach, a short ride.

My eyes focused on the view; my heart focused on the
joy around me as well as the beach that awaited.

Easing some of the uncomfortableness, I arrived.

My heart journal filling up with new pages.

Swimming in the water, I reunited with the soothing touch of waves.

In our lives, waves come and go.

Some soothe our soul; others cause turmoil.

Today, if waves come your way:

Set your eyes on the view; pay attention to
the beauty that surrounds you.

Give room to focus on your goal, and the power it offers to have one.

I noticed a mom and her daughter skipping along.

I couldn't hear their laughter; however, I caught sight
of their smiling eyes and giggling bodies.

The presence of a joyous moment transmitted straight to me.

This morning, I too gifted myself with a short session of skipping.

Within minutes, my entire being felt a rush of frolic festivity.

Introducing enthusiasm for my silliness, my life moment.

Today, enjoy a skip around the room; be enthusiastic about yourself!

It is yours.

The force that keeps your liveliness moving.

It is yours.

The heroism that continues to find a way into your moments.

It is yours.

The virtue that holds you high, gives you strength to go on.

It is yours.

The hope that makes the beating of your soul extraordinary.

It is yours.

Sit, rest awhile.

You deserve it!

You did it!

You marched hand in hand with courage!

You stood tall with your truth!

Your smile won!

You welcomed moments filled with compassion!

You did it!

You chose to let the light in when darkness came knocking!

You accepted a hand and offered one!

146

You gave gratitude a place in your moments!

Sit, rest awhile.

You deserve it!

You did it!

What a privilege it is to be you!

147

"Look at my eyes. Can you see them smiling?" I
asked my two-and-a-half-year-old grandson.

We practiced looking into each other's eyes in
an attempt to vanish the fear of a mask.

"Yes!" my grandson answered.

Showing me with pride how his eyes smile.

For a while, masks seemed to cover the language of a smile.

As I walked down my neighborhood street, the warm
welcome of smiles was nowhere to be found.

On so many occasions, smiles have connected us.

Entire heart conversations have been held
through the magic of a smile.

Perhaps the empty smile space has shaped room for innovation.

Creating a platform for a different way of communication.

One that has always been available but less used.

Our eyes!

On my way home, as I passed people from a distance, my eyes smiled.

While I was waiting at a traffic light, a set of
beautiful eyes spoke sweetly to me.

Eyes connected, a less-used language emerged,
opening the gates of connection.

Eyes have a depth to them, allowing a glimpse into the soul.

It may be that these masks have offered us a
new road to connection and intimacy!

Today, look into someone's eyes; hear their
soul speak; see their sparkle.

Romeo was my dog.

A small yet fluffy body seldomly shed his soft white-grayish coat.

He was one of my wisest teachers!

He was there when I learned to gift my soul the processes of shedding.

To consciously lose what blocked the beautiful view in my moments.

He sat snuggled up by my side patiently, as
meditation became my practice.

Adapting into my heart's home the beauty of stillness.

Moments of quietness can help us shed

what clouds the most exquisite views our soul offers.

It's been a number of years since Romeo and I softly said goodbye.

I smile as I remember his sweetness, holding his many lessons close by.

Spend a moment of quietude; shed a bit.

Enjoy your soul's magnificent view.

"What does 'savor' mean?" my granddaughter
asked in her soft, curious voice.

As I held her small yet growing hand in mine,
unexpected emotions halted my response.

As the soft flow of her breath covered my heart, I smiled.

This I savor!

Sitting here with you, our eyes writing infinite heart memories.

Knowing that your questioning is the next step on the ladder of hope.

This I savor!

Listening as you discover the beauty of reading,
as you delight in the magic of a story.

This I savor!

Sweeping your delicious hug into the arms of my soul.

This I savor!

"Savta, what does 'savor' mean?" she asked in her soft voice.

"To love exactly where you are, to enjoy with all your might.

"Just like I am doing now!" I added.

Her freckled face became one big smile. "I got it!"

What does "savor" mean to you?

152

My grandson has shown me many paths of wisdom.

Opened windows to scenes of life I had not yet witnessed.

A soul older than his years, a smile filled with childlike sweetness.

"How is your peace?" he questioned my heart.

Half a day later, after sitting closely with this self-
observation, I heard my heart's reply:

My peace comes and goes, always finding a place to rest.

She sways at times more than others.

There are days when my peace is found in every corner of my being,

and times that she hides quietly.

My peace caresses my soul with a sweet awareness.

153

How is your peace?

There is a room in my home.

For years, it's walls were a wine color,

covered with bookcases filled with books.

Two windows, one covered by a bookcase,

the other allowing the day's message to enter.

My work desk is comfortably placed,

giving me nature's view.

Lockdown presented me with innovative moments;

one of them was to renew the energy that
had lived in this room for so long.

The walls are now cream, pictures of my loved ones decorate a corner.

The covered window now shares the morning
sunrise and the evening moon.

For a long time, I had missed the fresh air and beautiful view.

The delicious new energy opened my heart window.

Sometimes, like in my room, we cover a window to our heart.

Not realizing the loving view others offer us.

Blocking the possibility of breathing in the air of connection.

Uncover the window that blocks the view to your heart.

Approximately thirty years ago, I received a recipe for a carrot soufflé.

An immediate love affair developed between
my family and this delicious soufflé.

Over the years, it has found a special place at our holiday meals.

Finding its way to the tables of family members and friends.

Creating connection with an orange sweetness.

This morning, as I took out two carrot soufflés from
the oven in preparation for Rosh Hashanah,

a moment of acceptance occurred.

This year, carrot soufflés would be on a different kind of holiday table.

Fewer places would be set; fewer knocks at the door would be heard.

Relying on the gifts of our family bond, our
celebration would be through screens.

Meaningful words that were once said to
me appeared in my heart's vision:

"It will be alright, just a different kind of alright."

Alright comes in different colors and different shapes.

Alright changes constantly.

Alright is a good beginning to the next wonderful moment.

Welcome the alright of your today!

From my carrot soufflé to yours, a hug.

Within the boundaries of distance our words met.

From different worlds, on a park bench in the land of the internet.

A lifetime ago, we shared a voyage of self-discovery,

hoping to share the beauty of diversity.

Each of us desperately trying to find balancing calm

amongst the chaotic waves of war.

"Breathe with me; I am holding your hand; you are
holding mine," her fingers slowly typed.

"For now, at this moment, we can slow down the pace; it is our
moment." I felt the keyboard entering my words on the screen.

The power of a moment delivering us both
the balancing calm we longed for.

This weekend, remind your heart of the power your moment has!

My father loved taking photographs.

As a child, I disliked his constant requests to stop for a snapshot.

Unaware then of the heart value a photograph could hold.

As I continue to travel on my newly discovered journey
with photography, I can sense his smile.

An image can hold a moment of awe, a moment of connection and joy.

It can cradle sadness or an instant of pride.

A photograph holds the past in clear view.

Photos have the ability to remind us of fears we have overcome,
places we have discovered, and loves we have experienced.

Awareness can be the camera of our heart.

Clicking intentionally on the scenery of our moments.

Gently placing the twinkle of an instant in
the picture book of our soul.

Meet up with your smile; invite your heart to dance.

I had never met her before.

As I walked at a slow pace tightly close to those around me, I saw her.

She stood on the side, holding a sign just like mine.

The weather was cold, yet she was dressed in a short leather jacket.

I wore a heavy winter coat, hat, and gloves.

As I came closer, she smiled at me, looking straight into my eyes.

Our reasoning for being there had a united message.

She wore her identity on her skin; mine was less obvious.

I stopped, thanked her for being there; without
much thought, I hugged her.

We stood like that for not more than a few
seconds, yet it felt as if time stood still.

As I pulled away, the tear on my cheek became obvious.

She softly said, "Of course we are here," wiping her tear away.

There is an immensity about the morning!

It shows up.

It is the beginning, appearing over and over again.

Standing tall with all its possibilities.

The morning holds a pearl of wisdom so great and clear.

It shows up every day of our lives, hoping we will take in all it offers.

No matter how hard the prior day seemed, how difficult
the struggle can be, the morning shows up!

The sun rises; the moon disappears.

It is universal.

It shows up!

It lives as if it were the whole world.

Perhaps the lesson to be learned is that one must care
for her soul as if she, too, were the whole world.

I can clearly remember that moment.

When discovery and magic met.

Realizing that around the world something was always happening!

As a little girl uncovering this fascinating truth, I was
eager and hungry to discover the wonders of life.

This is when I started the journey to my heart.

Only at a later time did I discover the magic of stillness.

Finding an opening door, an invitation to touch, see, and feel.

Be still for a moment; let your inner light
illuminate the answers your soul knows.

164

The winds are very strong this morning.

A view from my window shows a birdless sky.

Vibrating sounds indicating the power nature holds.

You, too, have vibrating sounds, coming
from your heart, from your soul.

They carry messages of passion, determination,
and faith in all you have to offer.

Hear, feel them, participate fully in what today has to offer.

Fall in love with your beautiful sounds from within!

The season has changed here in New York.

There is less color in my garden with many brown leaves.

Yet, on my rosebush, there are flowers that don't
want to flow with the change of season.

This particular rose has lasted for a while, fighting the
winds that seem to blow her fellow roses away.

She isn't as big as the roses that preceded her earlier in the season.

However, her persistence to stay proclaims a powerful strength.

Her shade of pink isn't as deep, although the
sweetness of her color is quite apparent.

Signs of age are seen on her petals, introducing a new kind of beauty.

She sits strong, her petals fully open, announcing, *Here I am!*

Let your colors, your courage, your beauty, and your
strength introduce you as you declare, *Here I am!*

166

She was a survivor, not a fan of tears.

Tears were a sign of weakness, showing the
absence of courage and bravery.

For her, life was about survival.

Tears stood in the way of survival.

With each new grandchild, I noticed she allowed a tear to be seen.

Their tender and innocent souls invited her tears
to flow through slowly opening windows.

Windows that had been shut for years.

I recall on one very quiet day, we sat by ourselves, she in her
favorite recliner, I on her brown leather couch by her side.

I dared to ask the questions that were partly forbidden.

167

Hoping to fill the gaps in her painful story and pass them on to
her heritage, her grandchildren, her great-grandchildren.

Her beautiful hand, nails so perfectly polished,
held by my small, short-nailed fingers.

"Why don't you put nail polish on? It's important!"
Words I had become accustomed to hearing.

She sat silently; perhaps she knew her answers would
release the tears I saw desperately trying to escape.

Finally understanding how looking "neat and
pretty" was of such importance to her.

We sat holding hands, the somber quiet filling
the room with so many words.

Her soft tears enabling a unique intimacy.

Allowing a tear to roll down your face can be liberating;
holding it back, you lose a possible moment of freedom.

I hope she felt some freedom.

We all have words of self-wisdom sitting
comfortably in our hearts and souls.

Exercising our spirit to hear them is a ritual that
awakens us to the core of who we are.

Light a candle; find a moment or two that allows you a bit of serenity.

Write down five words that describe you today.

Who you are now, not who you were yesterday
or who you will be tomorrow.

Tap into the core of your soul, and listen to who you are.

Close your eyes for just a few moments.

Envision yourself without the interferences of your day.

All else has evaporated; only you remain in the room.

Perfect just as you are.

Flawless!

What would you choose to do?

No need to envision one thing; envision hundreds.

Deep within your gut, feel it.

Invite love, passion, and life!

As you slowly open your eyes, let the hidden treasure of you emerge.

Their children with grieving eyes told me of his last beach visit.

With great strength, she pushed her husband's
wheelchair onto the deep sand.

He had waited for this day with great excitement.

Twenty-five years he dreamed of being on the beach.

Twenty-five years he dreamed of entering the ocean.

As the waves welcomed them, they approached the ocean.

With helping hands and a special chair, he became one with the water.

His dream was fulfilled; their tears merged softly with the ocean.

What are your dreams?

When was the last time you tapped into them?

Reconnect with your dreams; help someone fulfill theirs.

171

172

We sat looking at each other.

She in her stillness, I in mine.

She is new to the family of rabbits in my yard.

This was the first time that I saw her adventure out by herself.

I knew if I moved, it would startle her; I knew if I spoke, she would run.

So we quietly stayed in place.

Without plan my eyes closed, and I chose that spot
for my morning moments of meditation.

Softly opening my eyes, taking in the sereneness of my
morning, I saw her hopping around close by.

Perhaps my stillness offered her safety.

Perhaps her stillness offered me serenity.

Share a moment of stillness, and see what follows.

She is dressed in white, her sparkling silver
hair falling softly on her shoulders.

I have seen her many times.

She is a greeter.

Standing by the entrance to the synagogue,
waiting with a friendly smile.

I don't know her name; I have never conversed with her.

We have shared many meaningful hugs.

The kind of hugs that are strong yet gentle, seem endless yet are short.

In my mind, she is a woman of hugs.

I find myself excited each time we approach the entrance to the
synagogue, knowing the hug woman will be there to greet me.

173

I don't know her name; I have never conversed with her.

Yet her hugs move me to soft tears.

The power of a silent hug should never be underestimated.

We met last night for the first time in forty-two years.

He was part of a group of friends that I had spent a year
with on my first adventure away from home.

174

He came dressed quite neatly, with a nice blazer and serious overcoat.

The short-hair part of his unfamiliar distinguished look.

Yet his smile and laughter were incredibly familiar.

I listened as he shared his now, his past,
and his concerns for the future.

We laughed a lot!

We shared sad moments, compassion, and hope.

We were young, forty-two years ago, discovering
independence and freedom.

Back then, he seemed uninterested in life's mysteries.

Quietude and love for solitude are how I remembered him.

Last night, his voice was strong with
determination, positivity, and love.

One of an adoring father.

Perhaps it was that my heart heard his words, this time.

Many people join us on our paths of life; what a gift it is to have
a second chance to learn the lessons they have to offer us.

He sits close to the curb on the east side of the crossway.

Covered by a multicolored blanket in a half-hidden wheelchair.

I don't know his name.

In front of him is a small neighborhood bodega.

My favorite place to buy flowers.

As the weather has gotten colder, his layers have increased.

I have offered him food and quietly presented him with daily coins.

I don't know his name.

He has always graciously thanked me with a big sweet smile.

However, it is the times that I wave and loudly say,
"Hi! How are you today?" that his entire being seems
to glow, wrapped in the rainbow of his blanket.

We exchange a few words, just enough for him to blow me a kiss.

I don't know his name.

Today I will find out.

Tears gracefully dotted my cheekbones.

As I was sitting in one place, my belly muscles
were presented with a delightful workout.

A sweet pause allowed me to catch my breath.

In the land of Zoom, I was on a date with my laughing partners.

I was wrapped up in a bow of glorious bliss—a
timeless moment of joy filled my heart space!

Laughing partners are a gift.

Dancing with you as the music of a good belly laugh plays.

Soul connections are strengthened.

Our shared laughter embraced us in the hug we have missed.

Today, dance with a laughing partner to
the tune of a hearty belly laugh.

Celebrations need not a reason, other than life.

This past week, I sent a dear person a bouquet of flowers.

Arriving at the door, for no known reason.

An unexpected celebration of her, a bond,
a love, a connection of hearts.

Sometimes the best expectations are the ones we don't have.

Making it possible to celebrate life, not just live it.

As turbulent waves of disbelief, heartache, and sadness
shocked my being, I turned to my breath.

As I watched the news, pictures crossed the screen, painful
scenes of violence and hatred dashed with no sense of time
through my soul's album, I turned to my breath.

As voices of despair were heard waking up ghastly sounds of the past,

I turned to my breath.

As I checked in with others, and they with me, I turned to my breath.

Today, and every day, it is there for you, the power of your breath.

There is a light.

Sometimes it is impossible to recognize.

Sometimes it is hidden.

There is a light.

Sometimes it is in reach.

Sometimes it is so bright, the clarity is shocking.

There is a light.

Sometimes it illuminates your entire soul.

Sometimes it clears away the darkness of the night.

There is a light.

Sometimes it is shared by others.

Sometimes it is all for you.

There is a light.

Sometimes it sparkles with pride.

Sometimes its glow is subtle.

There is a light.

May a new dimension of gratitude find you.

In a timeworn green box sits an assortment of stamps.

While I was cleaning a shelf last week, it softly fell into my hands.

Awakening my heart ears to hear his familiar Cuban accent.

My father collected stamps.

He would sit in his familiar silence in his
familiar space, placing each stamp

precociously in its place.

His gentle hands guided by small silver tweezers.

As a little girl with long red hair, blue eyes, and a freckled
face, I would watch him quietly from afar.

Admiring his dedication and ability to embrace a passion
filled with bits of perfection and much calmness.

184

I never got to ask him about his love for stamps; my heart memory
believes it was a way of finding peace in the midst of life's chaos.

I like to think that my passion for moments of calm
stillness was a gift he passed on to me.

As I placed the slightly worn green box back in its place, I
was grateful for the everlasting connection it offered me.

Find your moments of gratitude for those
who have filled your heart space.

As a little girl, I would count the number of people I knew.

I found it fascinating, how my list of names continued to grow.

I loved the fact that there was no ending in sight to what I had begun.

My focus was never on concluding, or reaching completion,

but rather on enjoying the excitement of a thriving beginning.

There is something deliciously charming in
knowing there is no finish point.

Things to learn, people to meet, hands to hold.

A world to explore, ideas to create, hearts to embrace.

Set aside the worry of finishing; pamper your heart
moments with the charm of beginnings.

A year ago, hugs began drifting away like white clouds before a storm.

Having so sweetly decorated our heart skies with the softness of touch.

My embrace learned to position itself from a distance.

Keeping available hugs on grateful alert.

This past week, a rainbow of hugs has
returned to the skies of my heart.

Filling my soul like joyous cottony clouds
dancing in newly born blue skies.

Tears quietly filled the close distance between our hearts.

We didn't forget; our spirits remembered.

The preciousness of a hug safely awaited us
in the treasure box of our hearts.

May the gifts of hugs always return to find a home in our moments.

From me to you, a hug.

A moment flashed by in a swift, surreal way.

Our united grasp released with no warning, separated.

Woods witnessing the brief second between letting go and holding on.

The mind quickly running faster than any limb could.

Voices in their quietness embraced with distant arms.

Nature refusing to let go.

With his vigorous determination, he held on.

As he dusted off the wet mud, it seemed as if he
were dusting off all that had occurred.

Hands clasped in a familiar love, we walked.

Knowing the sacredness of the second
between letting go and holding on.

Letting go and holding on, house different
meanings in the rooms of our souls

at different times.

Trust your heart wisdom to know which room to visit.

In my yard, there lives a tree.

It blossoms this time of year with beautiful flowers.

Decorating my view with the colors of spring.

I remember the day it was planted, joy filled my soul.

The tree was just a baby—no flowers, no fruit.

Today it stands secure and tall.

Sharing the wealth of its strong roots and beauty for all to see.

With much frenzy going on these days, this tree offers me quietude.

Granting me a keepsake of the joy that was,
the joy that is, the joy that can be.

Trust that the frenzy of every day doesn't need
to be the frenzy of your every moment.

Find your own quietude.

There is never room for bigotry, racism, or ill treatment toward anyone.

There is never room for actions of abhorrence proclaiming to be just.

There is never room for hatred.

There is always room for kindness.

There is always room for compassion.

There is always room for love.

There is always room for respect.

Allow room for all that can make the
moments of our world better ones.

May your touch always remember the silent language of kindness.

May your eyes never forget to share the vision of compassion.

May the words of your heart continue to tell
the story of empathy and loving care.

May a moment in your day be enhanced by the gentle
kindheartedness that humanity so softly holds.

A delicate soul I had met many times decided that
silence would become her best friend.

Tightening the soil around her soul, closing
herself in, as well as keeping others out.

Always having her compassionate ear available, slowly
forgetting what her own voice sounded like.

She made a brave decision and decided to start
loosening the soil suffocating her soul.

Moving layers and slowly revealing herself.

Plants need to be repotted every couple of years,
finding room for growth and new bloom.

Just as plants need repotting for growth, our souls do too.

She discovered many of her buried dreams, found
things that sparked her imagination.

Ways to accelerate her pulse, hear her beautiful voice,
and bring a smile to her unique and sweet being.

Does your soul need repotting?

There are so many good people.

Compassion shows up.

At times from the least expected people at the least expected time.

There are so many good people.

Kindness shows up.

Offered with no expectations.

There are so many good people.

Smiles show up quietly.

Sharing an exchange of joy.

There are so many good people.

Care and love show up.

Being given with no judgment.

There are so many good people.

There is an abundant amount of good all around you.

Last night I sat and listened.

I heard words of hope, words of prayer, words of grief and pain.

Last night I sat and listened.

I heard words of strength, words of determination,
words of courage and faith.

Last night I sat and listened.

I heard music conveying what the heart struggles to say in words.

Last night I sat and listened.

I saw tears that cried for change, compassion, and kindness.

Last night I sat and listened.

To the love offered by the beauty of diversity.

Last night I sat and listened.

Listen: open your heart to the gifts that sacred silence can offer.

195

We all have stories.

Stories we have lived and stories that were told to us.

We have created stories and been a part of stories that others created.

Stories we understand, stories that remain a mystery.

Stories are our memories.

Stories are the fortune and richness of our lives.

They contain wisdom.

Sharing your stories and the inner experience of life
with others offers a sacred inner satisfaction.

Share your stories: write them down, speak them,
sing them, draw them, dance them.

196

There is that one sentence or that one word.

The one that someone shared with us.

Someone we met only once, someone we knew well.

The words that never quite left our being.

Finding a home in our heart.

Reminding us to hear them when our soul
desires comfort and direction.

With the winds of uncertainty blowing, I yearn for the shelter of calm.

Finding it as stillness spreads her stormless wings around me.

Hearing the soft voices of gratitude and acceptance.

Embracing the whispering sounds of fear.

Surrendering, letting go, sweetly landing on the runway of life.

When my heart needs a rest from the
uncertainty of our times, I find nature.

When the unseemly fights its way to become reality, I find nature.

When humanity's shared beauty struggles to be seen, I find nature.

When I need to be reminded of the power a voice holds, I find nature.

In her beautiful embrace, nature sustains me.

Assuring a fresh breath, feeding my courage.

Gifting my soul with excitement and strength to reach higher.

Today, visit with the wonder of nature.

Remember all the good you are, all the good you create.

Your brave is big.

Your brave lifts you to heights of vulnerability, embraces
you with songs of compassion and nurture.

Your brave is big!

Your brave surrounds you with the wisdom of now, invites
your beauty to shine with a contagious rainbow.

Your brave is big!

Your brave is led by humor and love for your moment.

Your brave touched my heart, my soul, my being.

Your brave is big!

Sitting in a waiting room.

People from all walks of life.

In a matter of minutes, a community is created.

Stories of gratitude, love, and sorrow are shared.

A group of souls that have never met before and
most likely will never see each other again.

Pure concern, compassion, and care for fellow beings.

Sounds of laughter, quietly concealing heartbeats filled with worry.

A spontaneous community of kindness is created.

Paying no attention to religion, race, or gender differences.

Rather to the uniqueness of humanity that lifts the soul.

Today I hear love.

The sounds playing softly through me, the beat awakening my soul.

Today I hear love.

Unknown musical instruments creating infinite
tunes, my heart dancing to each musical note.

I hear love.

Today I hear love.

The sounds playing softly through me, the beat awakening my soul.

Today I hear love.

Unknown musical instruments creating infinite
tunes, my heart dancing to each musical note.

204

Today I hear love.

Over the years, various tunes and beats have
brought the sound of love to my being.

My listening skills improving over time.

Today I hear love.

Love needs no reason; its music can always be heard!

Listen, what does love sound like?

Her wide wings guided her.

High and then low, fast and then slow.

She circled, no flock following.

As she landed gently on the autumn sand, the
water continued to move ever so delicately.

Her stillness bringing me to mine.

A moment of tranquility in all its wisdom can guide you.

It invites you to be conscious without thought,

surrounding you with the miracle of being.

206

The door opened with determination.

His steps of pride could be heard throughout the house.

Small feet seemed to take gigantic leaps.

Arriving at my side, the enormity of his
sweetness seemed to erase his age.

Sounds of crackling clear wrap, impatiently waiting to be handed over.

The rose-like aroma filled my surroundings.

"Here, Savta [Grandma], these red roses are for you; I picked them out."

Joy in all its innocence, waking my heart moment
to a picture-perfect touch of love.

Flow with the innocence of joy.

Many years ago, I was taught how to pick a "good bunch of roses."

Feel the flower; it should be neither too hard nor too soft.

Neither fully blossomed, nor totally closed.

On my visits to a flower stand, I take my time, deciding
which bunch of roses will have the perfect bloom time.

I pay attention to matching the perfect-size vase to house the flowers.

Making sure the right amount of water is added.

It continuously amazes me how each rose at its own pace slowly opens.

Their beauty becoming more evident each day.

Every couple of days, I cut the stems, change the water.

Like roses, balance between the tough and the gentle, the closed
and the open, is needed to witness our own beauty and growth.

Making sure we have the necessary water to quench
the thirst our souls require to blossom.

Becoming the loving vessel that holds our soul.

Here in this book, every page is a beginning.

One that is yours to create on each visit.

In my moments of stillness, I have heard
your voices and seen your faces.

These words are for you:

May you always know that there is something
likable, lovable, and worthy within yourself.

May you awaken the desire within to discover your potential.

May you allow others to know you and your vulnerabilities.

May you explore the world, your soul, and the hearts of others.

May you always love freely and unconditionally.

May you always care for others and for yourself.

May you always know the miracle you are.

May you always know there is a heart that will forever
overflow with unconditional, eternal love and joy, for you.

From me to you, a hug.

ACKNOWLEDGMENTS

This book came to be because of all the souls who have brought gardens of inspiration into my moments.

With much thankfulness and appreciation:

To Stephanie, whose friendship helped me write my first Morning Inspiration.

To those who granted me the privilege to see them off as they sailed to new seas.

To the Morning Inspiration family that continues to share their room for joy.

To the women with whom I share a bond of friendship like no other.

To Gail Hudson, my editor who helped guide me with much compassion and understanding.

To my family:

The idea of this book spent many days on pages not written; it is with your unconditional love and embrace it was created . . .

To Maytali, Lironi, Yairi, Shaishai, and Adidi, my grandchildren, thank you for reminding me of the beauty of now.

To Ari and Jacob, who wholeheartedly cheered me on.

ACKNOWLEDGMENTS

To my awesome daughters . . .

Ayelet, you were the first to offer me the gift of a newly born hand and held mine as my heart words found their page.

Yonit, your enthusiasm continued to hug my heart with a contagious source of excitement.

To Netta, for without your constant words of encouragement, patience, and knowledge, this creation would have remained on pages not seen.

And to my partner in life and love, Steven, for always kissing me good morning.

Last but not least, I am deeply grateful for those who have remained unnamed but whose presence among these pages is an everlasting inspiration.

ABOUT THE AUTHOR

Susan, like each one of you, has a story. The chapters of her story continue to add pages, presenting an ever-growing passion for sharing the healing gifts of awareness.

As a young mother and wife, Susan studied creative drama at Kibbutzim College of Education, Technology and the Arts in Israel. After graduating, she developed and implemented an educational curriculum for creative drama at an elementary school before moving to the United States. Her evolving spiritual path led her to Chochmat HaLev, an independent center of Jewish meditation. While there, she developed a newfound passionate relationship with the power of spiritual healing, and in 2002 she became a certified Reiki practitioner.

Susan now offers spiritual coaching and care that is focused on, but not limited to, those touched by illness and loving someone through death. She also leads workshops and guided meditation sessions. In 2010 she began writing Morning Inspiration—An Email for Your Soul.

CPSIA information can be obtained
at www.ICGtesting.com
Printed in the USA
LVHW070247050122
707893LV00002B/30